Daughter, God Loves You!

"... for her price is far above rubies"
(Proverbs 31:10b)

 Dr. Cassundra White-Elliott

Daughter, God Loves You is a work of non-fiction; however, names have been excluded to protect all involved parties.

All scriptures are from various versions of the Bible, including King James Version, English Standard Version, New American Standard, JPS Tanakh, American King James Version, and Holman Christian Standard Bible.

CLF Publishing, LLC.
9161 Sierra Ave, Ste. 203C
Fontana, CA 92335
www.clfpublishing.org

Copyright © 2016 by Cassundra White-Elliott. All rights reserved. No portion of this book may be reproduced, stored in a retrieval system, or transmitted by any form or any means electronically, photocopied, recorded, or any other except for brief quotations in printed reviews, without the prior permission of the publisher.

Cover Design by Senir Design. Contact information- info@senirdesign.com.

ISBN# 978-0-9961971-9-9

Printed in the United States of America.

Acknowledgements

I acknowledge all the women of my life who ever gave me a word of guidance, whether I was wise enough to receive it or not. I thank all of you for caring enough to speak.

I acknowledge all the women of today who take the time to speak into a young girl's or young woman's life instead of turning your head and saying, "It does not concern me," or "She's not going to listen to me anyway." We must love our daughters enough to speak into their lives. We may not have given birth to them, but they are our daughters just the same.

Dedications

This book is dedicated to all the young girls and young women who are just beginning to get their feet wet with the true meaning of life.

To all who have already begun the struggles and the challenges of womanhood.

To those who have had eye-awakening moments and have wondered how to deal with them effectively.

To all who have ever felt as though they were alone.

God is with all of you. Read the pages of the book, and you will soon see!

Table of Contents

Introduction	7
Ch. One *How Do I Know God Loves Me?*	9
Ch. Two *Education, Knowledge, and Wisdom*	29
Ch. Three *Social Media's Impact ...*	41
Ch. Four *How Do I Deal with the Abuse ...?*	51
Ch. Five *What Does the Future Hold for Me?*	65
Conclusion	79
References	83
Gift of Salvation	85
About the Author	91
Other Available Books	93

Daughter, God Loves You!

Introduction

At forty-seven years of age, I stopped and took a look back to my past, remembering the days of my adolescence. I remember experiencing a quiet and peaceful existence. Yes, there was peer pressure. Yes, there was at least one drug in my neighborhood (marijuana). And yes, there were instances and opportunities for life-impacting situations to occur in families, in communities, in neighborhoods and everywhere.

When I compare my childhood experiences to what children, teenagers, and young adults are experiencing today, I am baffled at how the world has taken turns for the worse. I am equally as baffled, and horrified even, at the prominent and needless violence that is occurring in our land, in our communities and neighborhoods, and even in our families.

In the Bible, in 2 Chronicles 7:14, the Lord declares, *"If my people, which are called by my name, shall humble themselves, and pray, and seek my face, and turn from their wicked ways; then will I hear from heaven, and will forgive their sin, and will heal their land"* (KJV). It is time for the people of God to cry out loud, more than they have ever cried out before. It is time for the righteous to stand up and let their voices be heard. If we take a close look in our churches today, we will see we are losing a generation of youth. Sure, the senior citizens are there.

Sure, the middle-aged adults are there. And, sure you can see the young children there. But, we must ask ourselves, "Where are the teenagers, and where are the young adults? Why have they chosen not to attend worship services? Why does it seem that they have turned their backs on God? What is so appealing in the world that they would rather be out in the world than the house of God?"

Daughter, God Loves You was written to address some of the concerns that parents and other church members have regarding the youth of today and some of the challenges with which they are faced. We must stand and say no to Satan who wants to rob us of our children. The Bible declares, *"Train up a child in the way he should go: and when he is old, he will not depart from it"* (Proverbs 22:6 KJV). That one verse tells us that we have a responsibility to our children to train them in the admonition of the Lord. If we do what we have been instructed to do, we will not lose our children to the enemy and this world system. Sure, they may go astray for spell. But, we can rest in the Lord knowing that we have fulfilled our responsibility and that they will return unto the Lord in due season.

Chapter One
How Do I Know God Loves Me?

As a young girl or young woman, you may be secure in knowing your family members love you and care about your wellbeing. However, more important than the love of friends and family is having God's love. The love of friends and family can be conditional and may be temporal. However, God's love is everlasting and is unconditional.

The best way for me to help you understand God's love for you is to give you His Word. There are several scriptures below that will illustrate God's love for you, His child. An explanation for each scripture follows.

"Yea, I have loved thee with an everlasting love: therefore with loving-kindness I have drawn thee" (Jeremiah 31:3 KJV).

Those whom God loves with this love, He will draw to Himself, by the influences of His Spirit upon their souls. This means you will be so engulfed in God's love that you will draw near to Him.

"Since [you are] precious in my sight...and I have loved thee ... Fear not: for I am with [you]" (Isaiah 43:4-5 JPS Tanakh 1917).

Because you are precious to God, He will always be with you-- every moment of your life. You never have to fear being alone, for He is always present. Remember, God is omnipresent. He is everywhere at the same time.

"As the Father has loved Me [Jesus], so have I loved you" (John 15:9 NIV).

Jesus says as His Father loved Him, He in turn loves us. How awesome is it to know that the Lord and Savior loves you?

"Behold what manner of Love the Father hath bestowed upon us, that we should be called the sons of God" (1 John 3:1 KJV).

God loves you so much that He considers you His daughter. You were adopted into God's family when you accepted His son Jesus as your Lord.

"He loves us so much that, 'He bowed the heavens also, and came down'" (Psalm 18:9 KJV).

When Jesus saw the condition of man- in our fallen state- He asked His Father to prepare Him a body, so He could enter into the earth realm. He came with a specific mission- to save us from being lost eternally. He came to restore us back to the Father.

"And, 'He sent from above, He took me, He drew me out of many waters'" (Psalm 18:16 KJV).

When Jesus was on earth, He suffered a great many afflictions. Angels were sent from heaven to protect Jesus from harm. God does the same for us. The heavenly hosts are often sent on our behalf to do God's bidding, keeping us from harm.

"Behold, I have engraved us upon the palms of my hands..." (Isaiah 49:16 ESV).

When a person has a tattoo, it usually has a meaning associated with it. Each time the person sees the tattoo, he/she is reminded of the meaning. God engraved Israel- His chosen people- upon Himself to serve as a constant reminder of them. God has a tender affection for His church and His children. He is constantly reminded of our needs and us.

"I will never leave you or forsake you" (Hebrews 13:5 *Holman Christian Standard Bible*).

The promise given here was also given to Jacob (Genesis 28:15), to Israel (Deuteronomy 31:6, 8), to Joshua (Joshua 1:5), to Solomon (1 Chronicles 28:20). It is therefore like a divine adage. What was said to them extends also to us. God will neither withdraw His presence ("never leave thee") nor His help ("nor forsake thee") (*Jamieson-Fausset-Brown Bible Commentary*).

"For the mountains shall depart and the hills be removed; but my kindness shall not depart from thee, neither shall my covenant of peace be removed, saith the Lord that hath mercy on thee" (Isaiah 54:10 KJV).

The love of God to His people is an everlasting love; it always continues; it never did, nor never will depart, though the Lord may hide His face from them, and afflict them, still He loves them; whatever departs from them, his kindness shall not; though riches may flee away from them, friends stand aloof off from them, health may be taken away, and life itself, yet the love of God is always the same (*Gill's Exposition of the Entire Bible*).

"As the heaven is high above the earth, so great is His mercy towards them that fear Him" (Psalm 103:11 KJV).

The space between the heaven and the earth is seemingly almost infinite; and nothing can more illustrate the mercy of God, which reaches to the heavens, and is in heaven; though this is but a faint representation of the largeness and abundance of it, and which indeed is boundless and infinite: so great is his mercy towards them that fear him (*Gill's Exposition of the Entire Bible*).

"Many are the afflictions of the righteous. But the Lord delivers them out of them all. He keeps all his bones; not one of them is broken" (Psalm 34:19-20 ESV).

In the world you may have tribulation, and your afflictions and troubles may be many; however, in time, God will deliver you and relieve your afflictions.

"When you pass through the waters (trouble) I will be with you; and through the rivers, they will not overflow you; when you walk through the fire, you will not be burned; nor will the flame kindle upon thee. For I am the Lord...You are precious in My sight and I LOVE YOU" (Isaiah 43:2-4 *New American Standard 1977*).

As we walk through our life, we will undoubtedly face some challenges. At times, the challenges will seem to overtake us, but they will not. At times, we may feel as if though we are alone, but we will not be. God will be with us every step of the way, through every challenge and every storm. That is how much He cares for us.

"God commendeth His Love toward us in that, while we were yet sinners, Christ died for us" (Romans 5:8 KJV).

God kindly demonstrates His love for us, even when we were found unworthy, through giving us His son to die an unworthy death, in order to draw us back to Him.

"For God so loved the world, that He gave His only begotten Son" (John 3:16 KJV).

God's love for us is best shown by the mercy and grace He demonstrates toward us. He gave us grace when He decided to give us the opportunity to avoid the penalty for our sins. The debt for sin is death. Someone had to die to pay for the sins of the world and the sins of each individual. God could have required our own blood, but He allowed His Son to die in our place, shedding His own blood.

"...having loved His own which were in the world, He loved them unto the end" (John 13:1b KJV).

Our Lord Jesus has a people in the world that are his own; he has purchased them, and paid dear for them, and he has set them apart for himself; they devote themselves to him as a peculiar people. Those whom Christ loves, He loves to the end. Nothing can separate a true believer from the love of Christ (*Matthew Henry's Concise Commentary*).

"What shall separate us from the love of Christ? Shall tribulation, or distress, or persecution, or famine, or nakedness, or peril, or sword? ... I am persuaded that neither death, nor life, nor angels, nor principalities, nor powers, nor things present, nor things to come, nor height, nor depth, nor any other creature shall be able to separate us from the Love of God which is in Christ Jesus, our Lord" (Romans 8:35, 38-39 ESV).

During the course of our lives, we will experience a variety of relationships, including parental relationships, sibling relationships, same-sex friendships, opposite-sex friendships, and romantic relationships. Relationships because of their very nature will have their ups and downs. Sometimes, relationships are severed due to irreconcilable differences. However, our relationship with God cannot and will not be severed- unless WE decide to walk away from God. God, on the other hand, is fully committed to us. Remember, He has already told us that He will never leave or forsake us. There is nothing that we can do, or nothing anyone else can do, to make God turn His back on us.

You may have had a friendship that was severed due to someone else's interaction. Maybe someone lied to your friend, and as a result, your friend turned away from you. Well, Satan, our adversary, lies to God about us all the time. The Bible tells us Satan is an accuser of the brethren (believers). However, God does not allow Satan's lies to turn Him away from us. He loves us unconditionally. Nothing- absolutely nothing- can make God turn away from us.

"For the LORD is good and his love endures forever, his faithfulness continues through all generations" (Psalm 100:5 NIV).

Not only does God love us unconditionally and eternally, but also He loves the generations of believers that will come after us, just as He loved the generation of believers before us.

God's Perfect Love

Now that you know that God loves you unconditionally and without reservation, you need to know the benefits of God's love and how they will bless your life. According to the website, *AllAboutGOD.com*, God's perfect love begins with faith. Upon receiving His gift of love, we can have unexplainable peace, joy, and confidence in the worst of situations. We can supernaturally feel His loving arms around us when we need comfort, protection, or feel anxiety. It is by God's love that fear, worry, and the pain of rejection are removed; something that the unbelieving world cannot understand. The following verses will demonstrate the benefits of God's love.

"Strive for full restoration, encourage one another, *be of one mind, live in peace. And the God of love and peace will be with you*" (2 Corinthians 13:11 NIV).

Apostle Paul encourages believers to walk in the spirit of unity and to be peaceful with one another. If they do so, God will be with them and will love them and be at peace with them also.

"There is no fear in love. But perfect love drives out fear because fear has to do with punishment. The one who fears is not made perfect in love" (1 John 4:18 NIV).

When the Bible says to fear God, it means to have reverence for Him- to respect and love Him. We are not to live in fear of God's punishment for the things we do that are not pleasing to Him. We are to love Him as our creator, our provider, our comforter, our all in all, and not because He commands or demands our love because He does not. If we come to Him willingly, we will find that loving Him is as natural as loving our natural parents.

"See what great love the Father has lavished on us, that we should be called children of God! And that is what we are! The reason the world does not know us is that it did not know Him" (1 John 3:1 NIV).

God loves us so much that He considers us to be His children. The world does not understand this type of love from or relationship with a spiritual being. To know God is to understand His love. Understanding God is a result of having a relationship with Him.

Having a relationship with God can be compared to having a relationship with an adult who is not biologically related to you that you feel very closely connected with and see as a parent, or it can be compared to a relationship you have with a person your age that you view as a sister or brother. People do not always understand the connections we have to other people who are not related to us by blood or marriage. But, God allows us to be connected to Him and to others in a special way.

"Whoever does not love does not know God, because God is love. This is how God showed his love among us: He sent his one and only Son into the world that we might live through him" (1 John 4:8-9).

To love the children of God is to know God for one's self. If a person does not love God's children, he/she does not know God and cannot profess that he does.

"Therefore, there is now no condemnation for those who are in Christ Jesus, because through Christ Jesus the law of the Spirit of life set me free from the law of sin and death" (Romans 8:1 NIV).

Those who have not accepted Christ as their Lord and Savior will be condemned to spend eternity in hell's neverending fire. On the other hand, those who love God and have accepted Him as their own will not be condemned although they may at times be chastened for their disobedience.

"But because of his great love for us, God, who is rich in mercy, made us alive with Christ even when we were dead in transgressions [sin] – it is by grace you have been saved" (Ephesians 2:4-5 NIV).

Lost sinners are not simply sick people needing help; they are dead people needing life. The Son of God died that we might receive life through faith in Him (Wiersbe, 1991, p. 159).

"Keep your lives free from the love of money and be content with what you have, because God has said, 'Never will I leave you; never will I forsake you.' So we say with confidence, 'The Lord is my helper; I will not be afraid. What can man do to me?'" (Hebrews 13:5-6 NIV).

We are reminded of what has been said in other places in scripture: we are to have no other gods besides God Himself and, as God's children, we are to love one another. Furthermore, we are not to fear man, for man can kill the body, but he cannot take our soul. Only God can take possession of the spirit and soul.

God Loves You – His Loving Promise

In the letters to the first of the seven churches of Revelation (Ephesus), Jesus tells the local church to not forsake their first love—Him. He promises them *"… let him hear what the Spirit saith unto the churches; To him that overcometh will I give to eat of the tree of life, which is in the midst of the paradise of God"* (Revelation 2:7 KJV). Each address to the remaining six churches includes similar promises. Each church is called on to repent, therefore receiving the eternal blessings of our loving God.

He shows us that though we have [made and will make] many mistakes, He still loves us and gives us every chance to turn to Him. Because of His great and never-ending love for us, God wants us to benefit from and inherit all the good He has for us. He also promises that if we reject His love and gift of atonement through Jesus, we will face eternal hell.

God sent His Son to pay the price for us, so that we can be forgiven and saved from the punishment of hell. Jesus died in our place. This is not a reflection of an unjust and unloving God, but [it is] a reflection of our animosity and rejection of Him. Because He is a loving God, He provided the only way of escape.

No matter how many mistakes you have made, no matter how unworthy you think you are, He still loves you and wants you to come to know Him. If you do not yet know Him, consider accepting God's gift of love today. It has been paid in full for you.

God's Love Shown through Jesus Christ

Galatians 2:20: "*I have been crucified with Christ. It is no longer I who live, but Christ who lives in me. And the life I now live in the flesh I live by faith in the Son of God who loved me and gave himself for me*" (ESV).

As believers and followers of Christ, we live by the precedent Jesus set for us. If we ignore what Christ did (being born of a virgin, making disciples on earth, fulfilling the law by dying on a cross, and reconciling us back to the Father) and attempt to follow the Mosaic Law, we cause His death to be in vain.

1 John 4:9-11: *"In this the love of God was made manifest among us, that God sent his only Son into the world, so that we might live through him. In this is love, not that we have loved God but that he loved us and sent his Son to be the propitiation for our sins. Beloved, if God so loved us, we also ought to love one another"* (ESV).

Our love for others makes God's love real and visible to them, so we can better witness to them about Christ. It also makes God real and personal to us. Merely reading the Bible about God's love is not enough. Seek to experience that love in your heart by sharing it with others (Wiersbe, 1991, p. 226).

God Loves and Cares For Us

Zephaniah 3:17: *"The LORD your God is in your midst, a mighty one who will save; he will rejoice over you with gladness; he will quiet you by his love; he will exult over you with loud singing"* (ESV).

God will rejoice over His children with gladness, take us in His arms and quiet us with His love.

1 Peter 5:6-7: *"Humble yourselves, therefore, under the mighty hand of God so that at the proper time he may exalt you, casting all your anxieties on him, because he cares for you "* (ESV).

By nature, we do not want to submit to others. The phrase "clothed with humility" reminds us of Jesus when He wore a towel and washed Peter's feet (John 13:1-11). If we are submitted to the Lord, we will submit to His people. Humility leads to honor; pride leads to shame (Wiersbe, 1991, p. 218).

Job 34:19: *"Who shows no partiality to princes, nor regards the rich more than the poor, for they are all the work of his hands?"* (ESV).

God does not favor one group of people over the other. He does not love the rich and hate the poor. He does not love whites and hates blacks. He does not love the educated and hate the uneducated. He does not love the successful and hate the unsuccessful. God loves all His children the same.

Psalm 86:15: *"But you, O Lord, are a God merciful and gracious, slow to anger and abounding in steadfast love and faithfulness"* (ESV).

King David is speaking here about God's qualities. It is important to know the God we serve. We need to know His characteristics and the depth of His love for us. Why serve a god you do not know? How can you know Him? Spend time with Him- read His Word and get to know Him.

What God Says About Love

Deuteronomy 7:9: *"Know therefore that the LORD your God is God, the faithful God who keeps covenant and steadfast love with those who love him and keep his commandments, to a thousand generations"* (ESV).

God is not a man who lies. If He promises something in His Word, He will ensure that it will come to pass. Trust in His Word.

Proverbs 8:17: *"I love those who love me, and those who seek me diligently find me"* (ESV).

If you love God with a pure heart and seek Him, you will surely find Him.

Jeremiah 29:11: *"For I know the plans I have for you, declares the LORD, plans for welfare and not for evil, to give you a future and a hope"* (ESV).

God only wants the best for you. The plans He has for you are good and will not cause you harm. However, in order to receive the good that God has for you, you must make the right choices. Have you ever been confused about the choices you should make? The more you read God's Word, it will begin to become clearer and clearer about what God wants and expects. He has given you free will to choose your own path, but He said He set before you good and evil, choose good.

John 13:34-35: *"A new commandment I give to you, that you love one another: just as I have loved you, you also are to love one another. By this all people will know that you are my disciples, if you have love for one another"* (ESV).

The distinguishing mark of true disciples is their love for one another (I John 2:7-11), and it is the kind of love that the world can see. He commands us to love, and He gives us the power to obey (Romans 3:5) (Wiersbe, 1991, p. 85).

Chapter Two
Education, Knowledge, and Wisdom

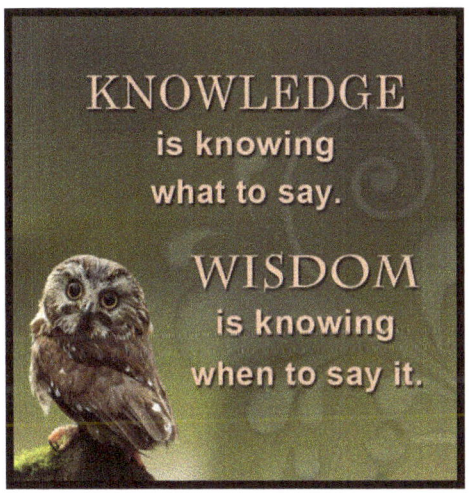

During a conference I recently attended, I had an opportunity to hear three teenage girls share their educational experiences, which had embedded in them a series of demeaning and thought-altering comments related to their abilities to excel in mathematics and/or science. One young lady shared her testimony, saying she excelled at math when she was very young, but she slowly began to realize she was the only girl excelling at math in her class along with a group of boys. Her realization made her uncomfortable. The uncomfortable feeling caused her to retreat from excelling in math because she did not want to be singled out or teased by her peers. Furthermore, no one encouraged her to continue with her apparent passion for mathematics despite her uncomfortable feelings.

For years, she retreated and did not allow herself to excel in math. Until one day ... things changed! The young lady met a woman who would later become her mentor. This woman encouraged the young lady to follow her passion. Today, the young lady is a junior in high school and is taking a pre-calculus class. In college, her major will be engineering. I take my hat off to this young lady for brushing past the stereotypes and to her mentor for encouraging the young lady to use her mind to achieve her desired goals.

Allow me to share a personal experience I had involving a similar situation. Approximately fifteen years ago, I was tutoring a young girl in math. She was really struggling to understand the concepts her teacher was attempting to teach her. One night at the end of our tutoring session, the young girl's mother said to me, "I told her it was okay if she does not excel in math because I never did either." My mouth literally fell open. I was both appalled and disappointed.

As parents and teachers, we need to look beyond ourselves and directly at the students' abilities. It is very possible that the little girl could have exceeded the level her mother did in math -- if she had a little encouragement. Instead, with her mother's comments, she felt it was okay to be substandard or mediocre. From my perspective, the mother should have encouraged her daughter to try hard rather than settle for the status quo. She should have allowed the end result to be whatever it turned out to be- naturally, without her interference.

Ladies, I encourage you to take Philippians 4:13 to heart: *"I can do all things through Christ who strengthens me"* (American King James Version (AKJV)). Taking it to heart means believing God uniquely designed you. He has a plan for your life and that plan may include a path that no one you know has ever taken or is presently on. Don't be afraid to step out the box and be different.

Allow me to use my life as an example for you. At eight years old, I began to have a burning desire to teach. At the time, no one in my family was a teacher, so I was not mimicking something I had seen through my familial relationships. When I attended junior and senior high, I excelled at math. I loved algebra, geometry, and trigonometry. One day, a family friend asked me what I wanted to do after high school.

I proudly stated, "I'm going to be a teacher."

He inquired, "Why not become a mathematician? You're really good at math, and you can make a lot of money."

I looked at him and was not moved because I knew what I had been called to do, and it had nothing to do with the monetary benefits. It was great that he encouraged me, but I needed to hear from God.

At that point in my life, I did not *necessarily* know that I needed to hear from God about my career, but I am glad I listened to the "inner me" because sometimes others can lead us astray whether they have our best interest at heart or not. My advice for you is- Let the Lord be your guide. I am not saying not to listen to adults who can mentor you because mentors are wonderful. And they can be very inspiring and instrumental in leading you in the right direction. What I am saying is to allow the Holy Spirit to guide you and do not allow people to push you in a direction you do not desire to go and do not let them stop you from a desire that is burning deeply inside.

The following testimony is an awesome example of a young lady who was not deterred from what one of her professors told her. This young lady did well in math and science when she was in high school, and she was the first one in her family to go to college. During her first semester in college, she was encouraged to take an overload of classes. 'An overload' means she took more than the standard twelve units that a student usually takes during a given semester.

The overload of classes caused the young lady to struggle and not do as well as she had desired. She went to one of her professors to discuss how she could go about successfully passing his class. He looked at her and told her, "I've never seen a pretty girl finish college yet." His statement was quite disappointing to the young lady. However, she did not permit his statement and the audacity he beheld to deter her from achieving her goal.

Two years later, she completed her AA degree. Then, she continued her education and achieved her bachelor's degree in Computer Science.

Today, she is a director of an IT department overseeing nearly 100 employees. She had no mentors and had received a negative comment, but she was determined to follow her dream. Today, she has proven to be successful and is now sharing her story with young people to encourage them to stay on the path they are on and to not be discouraged by any impediments that may come their way.

Whether or not you plan to attend college to achieve your career goal, you should be serious about the education you are receiving now (for those who have not yet graduated high school). Do not let peers or misguided adults lead you in the wrong direction. Take advantage of every learning opportunity you have.

Hosea 4:6 says, *"My people are destroyed for lack of knowledge: because thou hast rejected knowledge, I will also reject thee, that thou shalt be no priest to me: seeing thou hast forgotten the law of thy God, I will also forget thy children"* (KJV). This verse tells us when we reject knowledge, God will reject us, and we will perish.

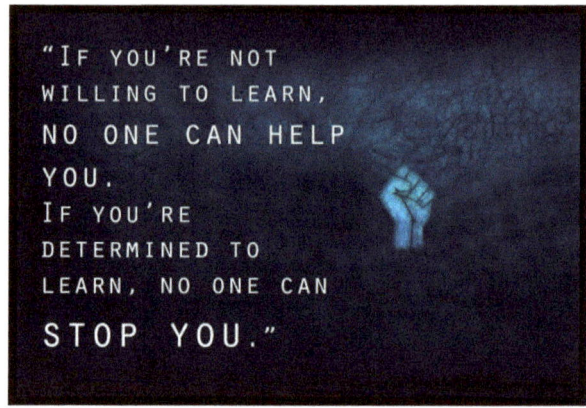

Here are some scriptures to give you a better understanding of what the Word says about knowledge and how important it is to have knowledge in your life.

Wisdom
Proverbs 2:10-11: *"For wisdom will come into your heart, and knowledge will be pleasant to your soul; discretion will watch over you, understanding will guard you"* (ESV).

When you allow God's wisdom to come into your heart, knowledge will fill you with understanding, keeping you from the dangers of this world and from walking in foolishness.

Fear of the Lord
Proverbs 1:7: *"The fear of the LORD is the beginning of knowledge; fools despise wisdom and instruction"* (ESV).

Of all things that are to be known, this is most evident- *God is to be feared,* to be reverenced, served, and worshipped, so this is the beginning of knowledge.

In order to attain all useful knowledge, we must fear God. We are not qualified to profit by the instructions that are given to us unless our minds are possessed with a holy reverence of God, and every thought within us be brought into obedience to Him.

Job 28:28: *"And he said to man, 'Behold, the fear of the Lord, that is wisdom, and to turn away from evil is understanding'"* (ESV).

Again, the fear that is mentioned is not a fear of God's wrath or of eternal damnation, but it is affection for God with reverence for Him. This affection is consistent with strong faith, great joy, and true courage; it is the opposite of pride and self-confidence and takes in the whole worship of God both externally and internally. It is called the fear of the Lord because He is the object and author of it. It is not from nature or in men naturally, but it comes from the grace of God and is a gift of it.

No man is wise until he fears the Lord, and when that grace is put into him, he begins to be wise, for this is the beginning of wisdom and is a principal part of it. It is very profitable to men, both for this life and for that to come (Adapted from John Gill's Exposition of the Bible).

Prayer for Wisdom and Knowledge
James 1:5: *"If any of you lacks wisdom, let him ask God, who gives generously to all without reproach, and it will be given him"* (ESV).

God is the giver of all good things; every good and perfect gift comes from Him, and therefore He, and He only, should be sought for all things we need. He gives to "all men" the bounties of His providence and to all who ask and call upon Him in sincerity. The riches of His grace, even to Jews and Gentiles, high and low, rich and poor, greater or lesser sinners, he gives "liberally," readily, and at once, freely and cheerfully, and largely and abundantly, not grudgingly, sparingly, or with a strait hand, but with an open one, and in a very extensive manner (Adapted from *John Gill's Exposition of the Bible*).

Biblical Example of Praying for Wisdom- Solomon
1 Kings 3:5-12: *"At Gibeon the LORD appeared to Solomon in a dream by night, and God said, "Ask what I shall give you." And Solomon said, "You have shown great and steadfast love to your servant David my father, because he walked before you in faithfulness, in righteousness, and in uprightness of heart toward you. And you have kept for him this great and steadfast love and have given him a son to sit on his throne this day. And now, O LORD my God, you have made your servant king in place of David my father, although I am but a little child. I do not know how to go out or come in. And your servant is in the midst of your people whom you*

have chosen, a great people, too many to be numbered or counted for multitude. Give your servant therefore an understanding mind to govern your people, that I may discern between good and evil, for who is able to govern this your great people?" It pleased the Lord that Solomon had asked this. And God said to him, "Because you have asked this, and have not asked for yourself long life or riches or the life of your enemies, but have asked for yourself understanding to discern what is right, behold, I now do according to your word. Behold, I give you a wise and discerning mind, so that none like you has been before you and none like you shall arise after you" (ESV).

Discernment
Daniel 2:21: *"He changes times and seasons; he removes kings and sets up kings; he gives wisdom to the wise and knowledge to those who have understanding"* (ESV).

An increase of wisdom and knowledge is given to wise politicians and counselors of state, to form wise schemes of peace or war, to make wise laws, and govern kingdoms in a prudent manner, and to wise master builders or ministers of the Word, to speak the wisdom of God in a mystery, to diffuse the knowledge of Christ everywhere. Likewise, God will give wisdom unto us to make wise decisions (Adapted from *John Gill's Exposition of the Bible*).

Psalm 119:66: *"Teach me good judgment and knowledge, for I believe in your commandments"* (ESV).

When we depend on God, we will trust Him to teach us good judgment, so we may rightly choose between truth and falsehood, good and evil. So, we may be kept from those errors in which many are involved and may clearly understand what God's law requires or permits and what it forbids (Adapted from *Benson's Commentary Online*).

Proverbs 16:22: *"Good sense is a fountain of life to him who has it, but the instruction of fools is folly"* (ESV).

Understanding is "a fountain of life" and gives health and refreshment both to the one who has it and her friends. On the other hand, the discipline given by fools is worse than useless, being folly itself. If fools refuse to be taught by wisdom, their own folly will serve as a rod to correct them.

Proverbs 1:5: *"Let the wise hear and increase in learning, and the one who understands obtain guidance"* (ESV).

A wise person is not self-conceited, as fools are, but willing to learn from others, and, therefore, will attend to instructions and will increase in her learning. Therefore, he will increase in knowledge and wisdom (Adapted from *Benson's Commentary Online*).

Ecclesiastes 7:12: *"For the protection of wisdom is like the protection of money, and the advantage of knowledge is that wisdom preserves the life of him who has it"* (ESV).

Wisdom is as good as an inheritance, actually even better. It shelters from the storms and scorching heat of trouble. Wealth will not lengthen one's natural life, but true wisdom will give spiritual life and strengthen men for service unto the Lord. When working for the Lord, be not conceited of your own abilities nor find fault with everything, nor busy yourself in other people's lives. Be concerned with yourself and your service to the King (Adapted from *Matthew Henry's Concise Commentary*).

Christian Quotes about Knowledge

The ultimate ground of faith and knowledge is confidence in God. ~ Charles Hodge

Wisdom is the right use of knowledge. To know is not to be wise. Many men know a great deal and are all the greater fools for it. There is no fool so great a fool as a knowing fool. But to know how to use knowledge is to have wisdom. ~ Charles Spurgeon

The Bible was not given to increase our knowledge but to change our lives. ~ D.L. Moody

Knowledge is power. ~ Francis Bacon

Knowledge is but folly unless it is guided by grace. ~ George Herbert

Chapter Three
Social Media's Impact on Today's Society

In today's world, people connect with one another in person, via the telephone, and via the Internet. The Internet was designed to be a system whereby individual users could connect with one another and share data and/or access data. Since the Internet's inception, users' capabilities have increased exponentially. We now have what is known as Social Media sites, where more and more people are connecting every day.

According to Merriam-Webster, an online dictionary, social media is defined as "forms of electronic communication (as Websites for social networking and microblogging) through which users create online communities to share information, ideas, personal messages, and other content (such as videos)."

Listed below are the top fifteen popular social networking sites and the estimated number of **unique** monthly visitors to the site.

1 Facebook	1,100,000,000
2 Twitter	310,000,000
3 LinkedIn	255,000,000
4 Pinterest	250,000,000
5 GooglePlus	120,000,000
6 Tumblr	110,000,000
7 Instagram	100,000,000
8 VK	80,000,000
9 Flickr	65,000,000
10 Vine	42,000,000
11 MeetUp	40,000,000
12 Tagged	38,000,000
13 Ask.fm	37,000,000
14 MeetMe	15,500,000
15 ClassMates	15,000,000

(Ebiz MBA, 2015)

10 Pros and Cons of Social Media

The Internet has changed the way we communicate and interact with one another on so many levels. Therefore, it is necessary to explore the pros and cons of Social Media and its effects on our society.

The Pros

1- Increased criminal prosecution because of Social Media

The NYC police department began using Twitter back in 2011 to track criminals foolish enough to brag about their crimes online. When the Vancouver Canucks lost the Stanley Cup in 2011, their Vancouver fans took to the streets and rioted, but local authorities used social media to track and tag the people involved, and they caught people who were stealing during the riot.

2- Social networking creates new social connections.

Statistics show that 70% of adults have used social media sites to connect with relatives in other states, and 57% of teens have reported making new friendships on social media sites.

Social networking is an extension of teens' real-world friendships. It helps them enrich and manage their social lives. Socializing online can give shy, socially awkward teens a comfortable way to communicate -- one that is less intimidating than meeting face-to-face. This can boost their self-esteem and help them practice their social skills (Stanberry, 2011).

3- Students are doing better in school

Students with Internet access at a rate of 50% have reported using social networking sites to discuss schoolwork, and another 59% talk about instructive topics.

4- Better quality of life
Members of support groups discuss their health conditions, share important information, and resources relevant to their conditions while creating strong support networks.

5- Social media as a source of employment
Job sourcing has gone modern thanks to social media. Sites such as LinkedIn are a major resource that 89% of job recruiters take advantage of when looking to hire potential employees.

<u>The Cons</u>
1- Social media and the news
Much of the news information that people read about comes from social media websites, and that figure estimate is around 27.8%. This figure ranks just under print newspapers at 28.8%, greater than radio's figure of 18.8% and far outpaces the figure for other print publications at just 6%.

2- Too much misinformation
With the advent of the web, people started to create their own websites and blogs. While many of those blogs were just basic diaries, a few of them were about topics like health and politics while others were *how to* blogs.
Many blogs have turned into rumor mills, spreading misinformation that people tend to believe just because it is on the web. For example, rumors about Hurricane

Sandy and gunfights in other countries, like Mexico, have been picked up by reliable news services, and this misinformation has been shared without the proper vetting of the sources providing the information.

3- Students who spend too much time on social media sites have lower academic grades.

Statistics show that students using social media too often tend to have GPA's of 3.06 compared to GPA's of 3.82 for pupils who don't use social media. An even scarier fact is that students who use social media tend to score 20% lower on their test scores than their counterparts.

4- Social Media sites to blame for lost productivity

Social media platforms like Facebook and Twitter are a direct cause for lost productivity at the workplace. In a survey, 36% of people said that social networking was the biggest waste of time in comparison to activities like fantasy football, shopping, and watching television.

5- Social Media is the cause of less face-to-face communication.

One last discussion about the pros and cons of social media is a lack of one-on-one communication. In a 2012 study, families who reported spending less time with one another *rose* from a level of 8% in 2000 to 32% in 2011. The study also reported that 32% of the people in the survey either were texting or were on social media sites instead of communicating with each other during family gatherings (Top Ten Social Media).

6- Online bullying and harassment by peers, also known as cyberbullying.
This may be the biggest online danger to kids. It's often an extension of bullying that takes place at school but can be just as damaging, if not more so (Stanberry 2011).

7- Online predators. While being harassed or stalked online by adult predators is far less common than cyberbullying, any incident is one too many (Stanberry, 2011). Predators disguise themselves as teenagers who seemingly fit into the same age group as the user and create a profile of the same interests for the single purpose of attracting the attention of the young lady. Before long, after a time of interacting with the young lady, the predator offers to meet her in a public or secluded place. The young lady, who is intrigued by the attention she is getting, agrees to meet him, and it is downhill from there.

A Message for Parents of Teenagers

The phenomenon of social networking has taken today's youth culture by storm. At the same time, it has raised serious concerns among the parents of these tech-savvy teens. Media reports of online predators, cyberbullies, ruined reputations, and other dangers have parents fearing the worst and wondering how to talk to their kids about the issue. What should a parent do? Teach your teen how to socialize safely online.

It is not easy to compete with your child's computer. She may consider Facebook her BFF, but it cannot give her love and guidance. However, you can. Try these tips from Kristin Stanberry (2011) to guide your teen's life online:

- Set (and enforce) reasonable rules and restrictions for your teen's use of online technology. For example, don't allow her to use her laptop computer in her bedroom, out of your sight and supervision. Just knowing you might walk by at any time may motivate her to be more mindful of the house rules.
- Connect with your child on Facebook or MySpace. If she's not crazy about this idea, point out that it could be a fun way to share photos, posts, and memories with cousins, grandparents, and other relatives.
- Be proactive. Educate your teen about the risks of social networking and how to avoid them. From knowing what to do if she's bullied online, or using privacy settings for her online profile, teach your teen to protect herself online.
- Coach your teen to use caution and common sense online. Remind her to think twice before posting comments, photos, or videos – all of which add to (or detract from) her reputation.
- Balance her online social life with face-to-face interaction. Encourage her to spend "face time" with friends, and keep family relationships strong by spending quality time together – and by simply making yourself available to listen and talk. Do not allow her to play with her smart phone at the dinner table; instead, draw her into the conversation and do your best to keep her engaged.

Give these tips a try, and fine-tune your approach as you work with your teenager to shape her social networking skills. If you succeed in some ways but not in others, don't despair! Raising a teenager – even one more tech-savvy than you are – is still something you are well-equipped to do.
(Stanberry, 2011)

Daughter, God Loves You!

Chapter Four
How Do I Deal with the Abuse I Have Suffered?

Unfortunately, abuse is not restrictive of age. Abuse can be inflicted upon anyone from the unborn child to the elderly. Also, abuse comes in a variety of forms, including verbal, mental, emotional, physical, financial, and sexual. Therefore, parents, guardians, leaders in the church, school officials, and law enforcement agents must be cognizant of abuse victims and how to care for their needs. Furthermore, abuse victims must be encouraged to speak out about what they have endured, so they may get the assistance in healing and recovery they so desperately need- even when they do not know they need it, or when they do not or cannot admit they need it.

It is imperative to their future and the future of their families that they get help in dealing with the effects of abuse, which can range from depression, suicidal ideations, promiscuity, anger, bitterness, mood swings, altered personality, split personality disorder, anorexia, bulimia, etc. The catastrophic list of effects is presumably endless.

This chapter will offer help to those who have suffered abuse and provide information for others in how to deal with abuse victims.

Domestic Abuse

Question: "What is the biblical perspective on domestic violence?"

Answer: Domestic violence is narrowly defined as an act or threatened act of violence upon someone with whom the perpetrator is or has previously been in intimate relationship. The term *domestic violence* often brings to mind the concept of the "battered wife" or perhaps a married couple's verbal argument escalating into physical assault. Domestic violence is also commonly linked to child abuse. Even if the children are not physically injured, watching or hearing a parent being abused can have severe psychological implications.

Domestic violence is about power and control. Though the term *violence* has physical connotations, domestic violence or abuse can occur in non-physical ways. For instance, abusers may manipulate their victims through emotional or economic means. Verbal abuse and sexual abuse are other forms. A person of any age, gender, socio-economic class, education level, or religion can be impacted by domestic violence.

Domestic abuse can be viewed in terms of a "cycle of violence." Tension builds; the victim attempts to keep the abuser calm, but eventually, an incident occurs. The abuser apologizes and attempts to make it up to the victim, perhaps by promising it will never occur again or by lavishing the victim with gifts. Then comes a period of calm before the tension begins to build again. The stages of this cycle may take only minutes or may develop over years. Without intervention, the periods of "making up" and "calm" often disappear.

Domestic violence is in stark opposition to God's plan for families. Genesis 1 and 2 depict marriage as a one-flesh, helping relationship. Ephesians 5:21 talks about mutual submission. Ephesians 5:22–24 explain a wife's submissiveness to her husband, while verses 25–33 talk about a husband's self-sacrificial love for his wife. I Peter 3:1–7 gives similar instructions. I Corinthians 7:4 says, *"The wife does not have authority over her own body but yields it to her husband. In the same way, the husband does not have authority over his own body but yields it to his wife"* (NIV). The two belong to one another and are called to love one another as Christ loved us. Marriage/relationship is an image of Christ and the church. Domestic violence is a far cry from the character of Jesus.

Many teenagers and young women suffer domestic violence in their love relationships (whether with boyfriends or husbands), and it hurts the heart of God. He is not unmoved by its victims, nor has He abandoned them. His plan for human relationships—particularly

those among family—is a beautiful depiction of who He is. Family is meant to reflect God's love. It saddens Him when a home turns into a place of pain. God's desire for those involved with domestic violence—both victims and abusers—is healing and wholeness.
(Domestic Violence, 2015)

Surviving Verbal Abuse

Words are power packed! According to the Bible, the words you speak can produce life or bring death (Proverbs 18:21). Our words can create and they can destroy. What we say is vitally important.

Unfortunately, during times of disagreement, words are used as the weapon to cut the opponent's heart. Psalm 64:3 talks about those who sharpen their tongues like a sword. It goes on to say that they shoot their words like arrows and their arrows are bitter words. They shoot in secret at the blameless without any fear.

There are people who do not hit, beat, push or physically abuse and can be very nice people. But under certain circumstances, something seems to snap inside of them, and they become hurtful, mean, selfish, angry, and destructive with their mouths. The abuser needs help and must repent, but what about the one being abused? How can they shield their heart from the arrows coming from within their own household?

The Bible gives us the plan for victory, and regardless of what is going on in somebody else, you have authority over your own soul. Here are some Bible-based steps to take.

1. Base your identity in Christ and not someone else. Know who you are in Christ. As a Christian, you are the blessed, the redeemed, loved, complete, restored, and a joint heir with Christ.

2. Speak aloud the words God says about you. Words of cursing must be replaced with words of blessing, even if you have to do it yourself. The words you speak over yourself are more powerful than the words someone else speaks over you. Do not receive the abusive words as truth. Remember, anything spoken against you that opposes what God says about you is not true. Every word you hear creates an image in your thought realm. The Bible says to cast down any imagination that exalts itself against the knowledge of God (2 Cor. 10:5).

3. Do not hate the abuser. The person speaking the evil words against you is only the vessel the enemy is using to get to you. Once when Peter spoke to Jesus, Jesus did not rebuke Peter. Instead, He rebuked the source: Satan. *"But He turned and said to Peter, 'Get behind Me, Satan! You are an offense to Me, for you are* *not mindful of the things of God, but the things of men'"* (Matt. 16:23 AKJV). Jesus saw the value in Peter and gave him opportunity to repent.

4. Do not carry the lying words with you and meditate on them. If you do, your heart will never heal, and you will continually be opening a wound and playing into the enemy's hands. Medicate the wound with the oil of forgiveness, bandage (cover) it with the Word, and quit scratching it. Do not remove the bandage to examine the wound. Let it heal. *"You shall be hidden from the scourge of the tongue, And you shall not be afraid of destruction when it comes"* (Job 5:21 New American Standard 1977).

5. Do not return abuse for abuse. It is easy to become defensive and throw stones at the one throwing stones at you. This only escalates the problem and is never a solution. *"Repay no one evil for evil . . ."* (Rom. 12:17 ESV). Understand this. Verbally abusive people are usually people who have been verbally abused themselves. Hurting people hurt people, and they usually hurt the ones closest to them. Sometimes, it is because they know you love them so much that you will take the abuse and never leave. You become their release valve. That may be a reason for the abuse, but there is no excuse for abuse.

If the abuse does not stop, you must not allow the lying words of the enemy to destroy you. Grace is God's willingness and His ability to empower you to overcome anything that comes against you. And God's grace is available for every Christian. If abuse comes at you as a

Category 5 storm, God will empower you with Category 6 grace. Greater is He that is in you than the attack that comes from the world, or from the mouth of a friend.

So what I am saying is this. You may not be able to get away from the abusive person, but through love, forgiveness, and grace, you can keep the abuse from getting *inside* of you and you can walk tall with joy in your heart, living your life in peace and victory in spite of the storm that may be going on around you.

God has a plan for your life, and His plan does not include abuse or defeat. His plan is victory and peace. God does not want you to simply survive verbal abuse, but to have victory over it. Do not allow the words of someone else to dictate the joy and happiness within your own heart.

Do not allow the words of someone else to take you to a place of withdrawal or depression. Stand firm, stand up, and hold your shield of faith. It will quench all the fiery darts from the enemy. Your belief in what God says will override what anyone else says. And the strength of God's words will add strength to you (Ollison Ministries, 2014).

Physical Abuse

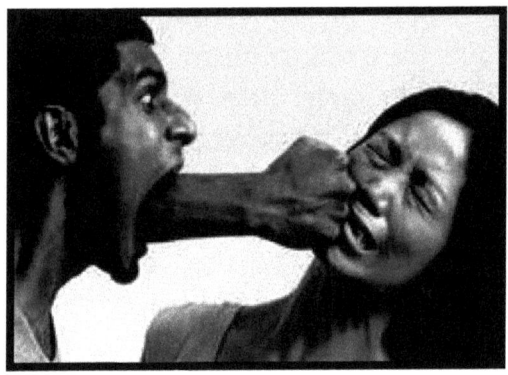

Psychological Effects of Physical Abuse

Unfortunately, some of the longest-lasting and most debilitating effects of physical abuse are psychological in nature. Depression is the primary psychological response to physical abuse but drug and alcohol abuse is also common. Abused women have a 16-times greater risk of abusing alcohol and a 9-times greater risk of abusing drugs when compared to non-abused women. Other psychological effects of physical abuse include:

- Suicidal behavior
- Self-mutilation
- Panic disorder
- Post-traumatic stress disorder (PTSD)

Effects of Physical Abuse on Children

Children are severely affected by physical abuse even if they, themselves, were not the victims of violence. It has been found that one-third of children who witness the battering of their mother demonstrate significant behavioral and emotional problems. The effects of physical abuse on children may include:

- Stuttering
- Psychosomatic disorders (disorders in which mental factors play a significant role – often vague complaints of pain)
- Anxiety; fears; compulsive behavior
- Sleep disruption
- Excessive crying
- Problems at school
- Depression
- Self-destructive behavior; running away
- Anger and hostility
- Low self-esteem
- Difficulty trusting others; relationship problems

Children who witness physical abuse are also more likely to be victims (often women) or perpetrators (often men) of physical abuse as adults.
(Tracy, 2014)

Sexual Abuse

www.stillwatersps23.com

Sexual abuse is unwanted sexual activity, with perpetrators using force, making threats or taking advantage of victims who cannot give consent. Most victims and perpetrators know each other. Immediate reactions to sexual abuse include shock, fear or disbelief. Long-term symptoms include anxiety, fear or post-traumatic stress disorder. While efforts to treat sex offenders remain unpromising, psychological interventions for survivors — especially group therapy — appears effective (American Psychological Association, 2016).

Sexual Abuse Categories:
- **Rape:** Forced sexual contact with someone who does not or cannot consent. Forcing sex upon someone who does not want it, who is intoxicated, or who is not legally old enough to

give consent all constitute rape. Though a handful of states specifically define rape as forcible sexual intercourse, any form of forcible sexual contact can have long-lasting effects on the victim, and most states now recognize forced oral sex and similar forms of assault as rape.

- **Child molestation:** Child molestation is any sexual contact with a child. Many children who are molested are too young to know what is happening and may not fight back. Some abusers use the child's cooperation in these cases as "evidence" that no one was harmed. Examples of child molestation might include fondling or demanding sexual favors from a child.
- **Sexual assault:** Non-consensual sexual contact with another person. Sexual assault includes behavior such as groping and any unwanted sexual touching. Attempted rape also falls into the category of sexual assault.
- **Other forms of sexual abuse:** Not all sexual abuse fits neatly into common legal or psychological definitions. For instance, parents who have sex in front of their children or who make sexually inappropriate comments to their children are engaging in sexual abuse. So-called revenge pornography sites, which publish nude photos of victims without their consent, are another form of sexual abuse.

How to interact with an abuse victim:

- **Believing loved ones who tell you they were abused.** There is no benefit to making a false rape allegation, and statistics consistently show that rape and other forms of sexual abuse are underreported. The rate of false reports for these crimes is also lower than that associated with other crimes.
- **Avoiding making jokes about rape or using rape as a metaphor for minor suffering.** "That test really raped me" can be triggering to rape victims.
- **Being mindful of triggering language and stimuli.** When you talk about sexual abuse, be aware of the fact that one or more observers may be victims.
- **Offering unconditional love and support to friends or family members who have survived an attack.**
- **Using language that the victim is most comfortable with.** Some prefer to be called survivors, since this highlights their triumph over the attack. Others feel that this language is patronizing. Be mindful of how you use language, and follow the victim's lead. A person who cannot say herself that she was raped may be made uncomfortable if you use the term to refer to his or her abuse.

(GoodTherapy.org., 2016)

Bottom Line of Abuse

Suffering abuse and dealing with the after effects can be an insurmountable journey. However, to walk in complete healing, there are certain steps you can take.

1. **Face the abuse.** The shame associated with abuse is unbearable. You can hide the pain for a season, but eventually, the wounds will surface. But take comfort, for God knows the horror that you have unjustly endured (see Psalm 139, Matt. 10:29-31). Ask God for the strength to face your nightmare of abuse.

2. **Forgive and release.** As difficult as it may sound, you need to begin by forgiving the perpetrator for his or her actions against you. It may seem impossible, but the consequences of unforgiveness can produce even further destruction (2 Samuel 13:23-29). Instead, ask God to give you the grace you need to forgive (1 Samuel 1:15-17, Psalm 42:3-4, Psalm 62:8).

3. **Seek shelter.** If you are still in an abusive situation, immediately seek shelter. Consider turning to family members, your church family, or perhaps authorities if necessary. Ultimately, rest in God's shelter. Turn to His Word (the Psalms offer much encouragement for the downcast).

4. **Move on.** Once you have taken steps to forgive, ask God to help you pick up the pieces, and seek again the abundant life in Jesus that He has for you (John 10:10). Press on and leave the past to God (Phil. 3:13-14).

(Christian Broadcasting Network, 2016)

Daughter, God Loves You!

Chapter Five
What Does the Future Hold for You?
(Being a Virtuous Woman)

The final chapter of the book of Proverbs presents a picture of what the future has in store for you- **IF** you decide to walk the way the Lord directs you. Not only does He want you to know that He loves you, He wants you to love yourself, be educated in all aspects of your life, be free from any scars of abuse you may have suffered, keep your eyes open to avoid potential abuse, and become a woman both you and He can be proud of.

God calls you His daughter *when* you call Him your Father. He is proud to be your loving Father. At the same time, He wants you to be a woman you can be proud to be, a woman who can hold her head up. The 31st Chapter of Proverbs gives a picture of what this woman looks like. As you read the following exposition of Proverbs 31 (adapted from John Gill's Exposition of Proverbs, except where noted), take in the various characteristics that form the sum total of the Proverbs 31 woman, a woman you can strive to be. Please note- as you read through, you may very well read some characteristics that you may not be able to identify with because of things that have transpired in your past. Remember, God forgives all acts of sin and unrighteousness. He wipes the slate clean. So, regardless of anything that may have happened in your life, you can still be a Proverbs 31 woman.

Proverbs 31 contains the instructions a mother gave to her son, a prince, whose name was Lemuel. It is unclear whether or not Lemuel and Solomon are one in the same, Lemuel being a pet name for Solomon. Nevertheless, the mother's words of wisdom were so valuable they were connected to the proverbs of Solomon. The introduction to her words is in Proverbs 31:1. The address to her son is in Proverbs 31:2. In Proverbs 31:3, she cautions her son against uncleanness and intemperance because of the deadly consequences they have to kings and to their subjects. A few of the other verses contain warnings as well. However, the majority of the chapter is dedicated to describing a virtuous woman, perhaps designed as instruction to her son in his choice of a wife.

Proverbs 31 (KJV) Verse-by-Verse Exposition
Verse 1. *"The words of king Lemuel, the prophecy that his mother taught him."* Whether or not Lemuel was an actual prince or Solomon himself, who may have been called Lemuel as a pet name by his mother, the words contained here were delivered as a foresight of the sins he would be tempted with and could possibly fall into. She wanted to prevent him from any mishaps he would possibly make.

Verse 2. *"What, my son? and what, the son of my womb? and what, the son of my vows?"* Although Lemuel was a king, his mother desired to speak to him as his mother, so she could offer words of advice to him. She wanted to ensure he behaved as a king and not as a mere man. She begged him to listen to her and her words of wisdom. She desired nothing from him, except that he tune his ear to hear and to obtain his full attention. She wanted to be sure he did not give his life over to wine and women. She also let him know that she was the son of her womb and that she had asked God for him and promised to dedicate him back to the Lord.

Verse 3. *"Give not thy strength unto women, nor thy ways to that which destroyeth kings."* The king was being cautioned to preserve the strength of his body, by not allowing it to be weakened by the excessive dealings with numerous women and to not give his mind over to take such paths or pursue methods that would bring destruction upon kings and kingdoms. The paths she was speaking of were such paths as having ambitious views of enlarging his territory by invading neighboring countries and making war with neighboring kings, to the ruin of them.

Verse 4. *"It is not for kings, O Lemuel, it is not for kings to drink wine; nor for princes strong drink."* Although it was lawful for kings to drink wine in a moderate manner, and for princes, counsellors, and judges to drink strong drink, it was very unbecoming for either of them to drink any of these to excess. Furthermore, it was very disgraceful to any man to drink immoderately, to make a beast of himself, and much more a king or judge, who, of all men, ought to be grave and sober. Sobriety was necessary so they could perform their office well and maintain the grandeur and dignity of it. Solomon, failing to heed the advice, gave himself unto wine as well as women (Ecclesiastes 2:3).

Verse 5. *"Lest they drink, and forget the law, and pervert the judgment of any of the afflicted."* Being in a drunken condition dumbfounds the mind and hurts the memory, and it makes men forgetful. A drunken king on the throne or a drunken judge on the bench is very unfit for his office because he renders himself incapable of attending to the cause before him or taking in the true state of the case. If he forgets the law, which is his rule of judgment, he will mistake the point in debate, put one thing for another, alter the judgment of the afflicted and injured person, and give the cause *against* him that should be *for* him. Therefore, it is of great consequence that kings and judges be sober.

Verse 6. *"Give strong drink unto him that is ready to perish, and wine to those that be of heavy heart."* It was suggested here to King Lemuel, and other kings and judges, rather than drink strong drink themselves, they should give it out liberally to poor persons in starving circumstances, who must perish, unless relieved, for it would do them good because they are pressed with the weight of their affliction and poverty: wine to such is very exhilarating and cheering, taking their minds from their circumstances.

Verse 7. *"Let him drink, and forget his poverty, and remember his misery no more."* The supposed logic is because the impoverished have situations that press upon them and afflict them, it is best to let them drink until they are cheerful and forget they are poor. If they forget (at least momentarily), they will not be troubled about it nor be anxious about having food and clothing. In a spiritual sense, those who are impoverished should be given the Gospel, which is as the best wine that goes down sweetly. They should be told of the love of God and Christ to poor sinners, which is better than wine; and the blessings of grace should be set before them, as peace, pardon, righteousness, and eternal life, by Christ, the milk and wine to be had without money and without price; of these they should drink, or participate of, by faith, freely, largely, and to full satisfaction; by means of which they will "forget" their spiritual "poverty," and consider themselves as possessed of the riches of grace, as rich in faith, and heirs of a kingdom; and so remember no more their miserable estate by nature, and the anguish of their souls in the view of that; unless it be to magnify and adore the riches of God's grace in their deliverance.

Verse 8. *"Open thy mouth for the dumb in the cause of all such as are appointed to destruction."* For those who cannot speak on their own behalf, either because they do not know the laws, or who are bashful, timid, or fearful, or do not have proper legal representation, Lemuel's mother advises him to open his mouth freely, readily, boldly, and without fear to plead for such persons, to ensure justice is properly carried out.

Verse 9. *"Open thy mouth, judge righteously, and plead the cause of the poor and needy."* Having heard the case of the poor, Lemuel was directed to give a righteous sentence, to deliver it freely and impartially, with boldness, not being concerned about wicked and unjust men. The poor are oppressed by the rich and cannot plead for themselves or pay others to plead for them. Therefore, it would be necessary for Lemuel to do it freely and faithfully. Thus, as Lemuel's mother cautions him against women and wine, she also advises him to do the duties of his office in administering impartial justice to all, and particularly in being the advocate and judge of the poor and distressed.

Verse 10. *"Who can find a virtuous woman? for her price* is *far above rubies."* This part of the chapter is disjointed from the rest (v. 1-9) because rather than give her son instructions for running his kingdom, Lemuel's mother describes the type of woman that would make a fit wife for her son.

"Virtuous" refers to one who is chaste in her love and affection to Christ, who would be her husband until she had a natural husband. The woman must also be steadfast in her adherence to Him by faith, as her Lord and Savior. She must be incorrupt in doctrine, sincere and spiritual in worship, and retain the purity of a disciplined and holy life. Also, the woman must be able to get wealth and riches by her wisdom and prudence.

Verse 11. *"The heart of her husband doth safely trust in her, so that he shall have no need of spoil."* She conducts herself so that he may have entire confidence in her. He trusts in her chastity, for she never gives him the least occasion to suspect or to entertain any jealousy. She is not unhappy and reserved, but modest and serious, and has all the marks of virtue in her countenance and behavior. Her husband knows it; therefore, his heart safely trusts in her. He trusts in her conduct, that she will speak in all companies and act in all affairs, with prudence and discretion, so as to not cause him damage or reproach. He trusts in her fidelity of his interests, and that she will never betray his counsels nor have any interest separate from that of his family. When he goes abroad, to attend the concerns of the public, he can confide in her to order all his affairs at home, as well as if he himself were there. She is a good wife that is fit to be trusted, and he is a good husband that will leave it to such a wife to manage for him. She contributes so much to his content and satisfaction *that he shall have no need of spoil*; he needs not to gripe and scrape while away on business because his wife manages his affairs so that he beforehand has such plenty of his own that he has no temptation to prey upon his neighbors (Matthew Henry's Online Commentary).

Verse 12. *"She will do him good, and not evil all the days of her life."* A good wife will repay good unto her husband, giving him thanks for all the good things he bestowed unto her. She will seek his interest and promote his honor and glory to the utmost. All the good works she does, which she is qualified for and ready to perform, are all done in his name and strength and with a view to his glory. She will not do any evil willingly and knowingly against him, against his truths and ordinances or that is detrimental to his honor or prejudicial to his interests.

Verse 13. *"She seeketh wool and flax, and worketh willingly with her hands."* A woman who is suitable for a wife does not wait until materials are brought to her to fashion them into garments. Instead, she seeks after them. This action shows her willingness to work. Her hands take delight in working.

Verse 14. *"She is like the merchant ships, she bringeth her food from afar."* A resourceful woman is not limited to the local areas for obtaining things she has need of. She is capable of going beyond her own boundaries to obtain that which she needs.

Verse 15. *"She riseth also while it is yet night, and giveth meat to her household, and a portion to her* *maidens."* A good wife seeks to make sure everyone in her household has food to eat. If it requires her getting up early to ensure the household is properly furnished, she will do it. She does not wait until the last minute to figure out how her husband and children will be fed. She attends to their needs before time, and she attends to the servants in her house as well.

Verse 16. *"She considereth a field, and buyeth it: with the fruit of her hand she planteth a vineyard."* She considers what an advantage a specific purchase will be to the family and what a good account it will turn to, and therefore she buys it, if it be worth her money and whether she can afford to take so much money out of her stock in order to purchase it and whether she has money at command to pay for it. Many have undone themselves by buying without considering, but those who would make advantageous purchases must first consider and then buy. She also plants a vineyard, but it is with the fruit of her hands; she does not take up money, or run into debt, to do it, but she does it with what she can spare out of the gains of her own home.

Verse 17. *"She girdeth her loins with strength, and strengtheneth her arms."* Showing her readiness to every good work, with cheerfulness, spirit, and resolution, she sets about doing it. She does all she finds to do with all her might and not in her own strength, but in the strength of Christ, to whom she seeks for it, and in whose strength she goes forth about her business, by whom the arms of her hands are made strong, even by the mighty God of Jacob.

Verse 18. *"She perceiveth that her merchandise [is] good, her candle goeth not out by night."* She is one that makes what she does turn to a good account, by her careful management of it. She does not toil all night and catch nothing; no, she herself perceives that her merchandise is good. She is sensible that in all her labor there is profit, and that encourages her to continue to work hard. She perceives that she can make things herself better and cheaper than she can buy them; she finds by observation what branch of her employment brings in the best returns, and to that she applies herself most closely. She brings in provisions of all things necessary and convenient for her family (Matthew Henry's Online Commentary).

Verse 19. *"She layeth her hands to the spindle, and her hands hold the distaff."* As the wife uses her hands to work, she thinks it not an action of belittlement, but one of power.

Verse 20. *"She stretcheth out her hand to the poor, yea, she reacheth forth her hands to the needy."* Her liberality is very extensive, reaches to many, and at a distance; it is done with great cheerfulness. She gives with both hands, liberally and largely.

Verse 21. *"She is not afraid of the snow for her household, for all her household are clothed with scarlet."* The wife will ensure those in her household are well covered from any storm that may befall them, just as the blood of the lamb covers and protects us.

Verse 22. *"She maketh herself coverings of tapestry, her clothing is silk and purple."* She makes herself coverings of tapestry to hang in her rooms, and she may be allowed to use them when they are of her own making. Her own clothing is rich and fine: it is silk and purple, according to her place and rank. Though she is not so vain as to spend much time in dressing herself, nor makes the putting on of apparel her adorning, nor values herself upon it, yet she has rich clothes and puts them on well (Matthew Henry's Online Commentary).

Verse 23. *"Her husband is known in the gates, when he sitteth among the elders of the land."* He is known to have a good wife. By his wise counsel and careful management of his business affairs, it appears that he has a discreet companion in his bosom. By conversation with her, he improves himself. By his cheerful countenance and pleasant humor, it appears that he has an agreeable wife at home. By his appearing clean and neat in his dress, everything about him decent and handsome, yet not gaudy, one may know he has a good wife at home who takes care of his clothes (Matthew Henry's Online Commentary).

Verse 24. *"She maketh fine linen, and selleth it, and delivereth girdles unto the merchant."* She not only seeks wool and flax and spins it, but makes it up into fine linen, which she then sells to advance herself and her family.

Verse 25. *"Strength and honour are her clothing, and she shall rejoice in time to come."* She wraps herself in strength and honor. She enjoys a firmness and constancy of mind and has the spirit to bear up under the many crosses and disappointments, which even the wise and virtuous must expect to meet with in this world. This clothing is for her defense as well as for decency. She deals honorably with all, and she has the pleasure of doing so, *and shall rejoice in time to come*; she shall reflect upon it with comfort, when she comes to be old, that she was not idle or useless when she was young. In the day of death, it will be a pleasure to her to think that she has lived to some good purpose.

Verse 26. *"She openeth her mouth with wisdom, and in her tongue is the law of kindness."* When she opens her mouth, for it is not always open, she expresses herself in a discreet and prudent manner. She speaks of things not foolish and trifling, but of moment and importance and of usefulness to others. She is discreet and obliging in all her discourse, not talkative, censorious, nor peevish, as some are, that know how to take pains; no, she opens her mouth with wisdom; when she does speak, it is with a great deal of prudence and very much to the purpose; you may perceive by every word she says how much she governs herself by the rules of wisdom. She not only takes prudent measures herself, but she gives prudent advice to others, not as assuming the authority of a dictator, but with the affection of a friend and an obliging air.

Verse 27. *"She looketh well to the ways of her household, and eateth not the bread of idleness."* She inspects the manners of all her servants, that she may check what is amiss among them, and oblige them all to behave properly and do their duty to God and one another, as well as to her; as Job, who put away iniquity far from his tabernacle, and David, who would suffer no wicked thing in his house. She does not intermeddle in the concerns of other people's houses; she thinks it enough for her to look well to her own and to take care of the concerns of her own home (Matthew Henry's Online Commentary).

Verse 28. *"Her children arise up, and call her blessed; her husband also, and he praiseth her."* Her children give her their good word. They are themselves a commendation to her, and they are ready to give great commendations of her. They pray for her and bless God that they had such a good mother. It is a debt that they owe her, a part of the honor that the fifth commandment requires to be paid to father and mother; and it is a double honor that is due to a good father and a good mother. Her husband takes all occasions to speak well of her, as one of the best of women.

Verse 29. *"Many daughters have done virtuously, but thou excellest them all."* While other women also prove to be virtuous, the wife Lemuel's mother describes will excel above them all.

Verse 30. *"Favour is deceitful, and beauty is vain: but a woman that feareth the Lord, she shall be praised."* A well-favored look, a graceful countenance, symmetry and proportion of parts, natural or artificial beauty, are vain and deceitful. Oftentimes, under them lies an ill-natured, deformed, and depraved mind; nor is the pleasure and satisfaction enjoyed as is promised along with these; and particularly they do fade and consume away by a fit of illness, and through old age, and at last by death.

Verse 31. *"Give her of the fruit of her hands, and let her own words praise her in the gates."* Some are praised above what is their due, but those that praise this wife give her that which she has dearly earned and which is justly due to her. It would be wrong if she did not have it. Note- The tree is known by its fruits, and therefore, if the fruit be good, the tree must have our good word. If her children be dutiful and respectful to her and conduct themselves as they ought, they then give her the fruit of her hands; she reaps the benefit of all the care she has taken of them, and thinks herself well paid.

Conclusion

According to Titus 2:3-5, older women have the God-given responsibility to teach and train younger women to be responsible with their husbands, children, households, and careers. The older must teach the younger to be keen, kindhearted, patient, respectful, and to be slow to speak, to judge and to anger. While teaching them temperance and the necessary life skills, mature women should not leave the younger to themselves to guide themselves or to attempt to guide one another. Mature women must always remember how it was to be young, foolish, and inexperienced. Young girls and young women must be guided into their destinies and God-given callings. Of course, the Holy Spirit is our guide, but God also gave us earthly guides who are endowed with wisdom. They have the wisdom to oversee the lives of those who are inexperienced and give them words of wisdom and encouragement, while admonishing them and giving rebukes when needed.

In this day and age, there is so much to be watchful for, such as Internet predators, unsavory characters looking for innocent victims, pedophiles, young boys and men looking for fertile girls who are not fully apprised of their "boys will be boys" personalities. There is more to be aware of today than there was a decade ago.

For those who are older, wiser, and more mature and fall into the category of guides, do not hesitate to ask God for wisdom about anything that may be questionable, unfamiliar, out or your realm of knowledge. For the young girls and young women who need guidance, do not get beside yourself thinking you do not need anyone to tell you anything. Older women have been where you are now, and many of them are where you are trying to go. When your head gets so big that you cannot hear from your elders, you need to check in with the Lord quickly for a reality check.

Young girls and young ladies, we are only here to assist in your growth and development. We are not trying to run your life or take anything from you. We simply want to enhance your life by sharing all God has blessed us to learn, experience and/or witness. Think about this- would it not be better to hear someone else's experiences about heartache, pain, and missteps rather than experiencing it ourselves? Sometimes, we make the mistake of wanting to do things our own way rather than using a proven and tried method. Be not wise in thy own eyes (Prov. 3:7). Lean not to your own understanding (Prov. 3:5). Sooner or later, we must stop kicking against the prick and take heed to wisdom (Acts 26:14).

If you are ready for a bright and prosperous future, now that you have read the book, find a woman you believe you can connect with to talk to, share the challenges you may be having, and to ask questions. This woman may be your mother, grandmother, aunt, older sister, teacher, someone at church, etc. Once you have chosen her, grab her by the hand and get ready for the journey ahead of you.

Be blessed in all you do. Always acknowledge the Lord, and He will direct your paths (Prov. 3:5).

Daughter, God Loves You!

References

American Psychological Association. (2016). "Sexual Abuse."

Benson, Joseph. (1857). *Benson's Commentary Online.* Biblehub.com.

Domesticviolence.org. (2015).

Gill, John. (1746-63). Gill's Exposition of the Entire Bible. Biblehub.com

"God's Love." (2002 – 2015). AllAboutGOD.com.

Goodtherapy.org. (2016).

Got Questions Ministry. (2002-2015). "Domestic Violence."

Henry, Matthew. (2014). "Matthew Henry Commentary on the Whole Bible."

"How to Survive Verbal Abuse." (2016). Larry Ollison Ministries. www.cfaith.com.

Jamieson, Robert, A. R. Fausset, & David Brown. (1882). Jamieson-Fausset-Brown Bible Commentary.

John Gill's Exposition of Proverbs. (2004-2012). Providence Baptist Ministries. www.pbministries.org.

"Keys to Powerful Living: Overcoming Child Abuse." (2016). Christian Broadcasting Network.

Larry Ollison Ministries. (2014). ollison.org

Matthew Henry's Online Commentary. (2014). Biblestudytools.com

"Sexual Assault/Abuse." (2016). Goodtherapy.org

"Social Media." (2016). Merriam-Webster Online.

Stanberry, Kristin. (2011). *The Pros and Cons of Social Networking for Teenagers: A Parent's Guide.*

Top Ten Social Media. Toptensocialmedia.com

Tracy, Natasha. (2014). "Effects of Physical Abuse, Pictures of Physical Abuse." HealthyPlace.com.

Wiersbe, Warren. (1991). *Chapter-by-Chapter Bible Commentary.* Thomas Nelson Publishers.

Gift of Salvation
for Non-Believers

"For all have sinned, and come short of the glory of God."
(Romans 3:23)

This section was written especially for non-believers, those who have not accepted the gift of salvation. The gift of salvation saves souls from eternal damnation and is a free gift offered by God himself.

John 3:16-18 says, "*For God so loved the world, that he gave his only begotten Son, that whosoever believeth in him should not perish, but have everlasting life. For God sent not his Son into the world to condemn the world; but that the world through him might be saved. He that believeth on him is not condemned: but he that believeth not is condemned already, because he hath not believed in the name of the only begotten Son of God.*"

This section of scripture tells us God's purpose for giving His son Jesus to the world. The world was in a bad condition. The world was overwrought with sin; the people were living for fleshly desires rather than for God's desires.

As a result of the world's conditions, God decided He would offer the perfect sacrifice that would save the world from being a place where people were lost and had no hope. He decided that His own son could stand in proxy for the sin-filled world, taking all sin upon Himself.

So Jesus came, born of a virgin, to save this dying world. He walked on this earth for 33 ½ years, doing the work of His Heavenly Father. At the appointed time, He died by way of crucifixion upon a cross at Calvary, on Golgatha's hill. He shed his blood and died for you and for me. Because His blood was pure, it paid the penalty for all unrighteousness and gave those who believe in Him direct access to His father's throne.

Scripture tells us in Matthew 27:51 that the veil of the temple was ripped in two from top to bottom, at the moment that Jesus' spirit left His body. As a result of the veil's removal, we are no longer required to have a high priest make intercession for us. We, as the children of the Most High God, are able to approach the throne God for ourselves, and Jesus sits on the right hand of the Father making intercession for us.

But what is even more miraculous than God offering His own son as the perfect sacrifice was the fact that when Jesus was placed in grave clothes and placed in a tomb, He only remained there until the third day. God would not have it that His son would remain in the heart of the earth forever. In order for people to believe in the awesome power of God and His dear son Jesus, a miracle had to be performed. So, on the third day, after Jesus died on the cross, He was resurrected, demonstrating the omnipotence of God. This very act was the act that would cause people to believe in a god that reigns supreme and holds the power of the universe in His very hands, a god that could save them from themselves.

Today, if you are an unbeliever, you can change your destiny. You can change where you will spend your eternity. Our Heavenly Father gives us the freedom of choice about how we want to live our life here on earth and how we want to spend eternity. In Deuteronomy 30:19, God boldly declares, *"I call heaven and earth to record this day against you, that I have set before you life and death, blessing and cursing: therefore choose life, that both thou and thy seed may live."*

So, dear friend what choice will you make today? Will you spend your eternity with the Creator or will you suffer Hell's eternal flames? Again, the choice is yours. Just as the men aboard the ship who were with Jonah became believers, you too can make a choice to accept the only one and true living God as your god.

If after reading the above passages, you have decided that you want to spend your eternity in Heaven with God, the creator, and His son Jesus, and the Holy Spirit, read through what has affectionately come to be known as the Roman's Road. This is the road to salvation. As you read through the scriptures that comprise the Roman's Road, you will also read the explanation for each scripture so you will have clarity about what you are reading and confessing.

The Roman's Road to Salvation

The road to salvation begins with Romans 3:23 which declares, *"For all have sinned, and come short of the glory of God."* This scripture explains that everyone has come short of God's glory and needs redemption. Then Romans 6:23a states, *"For the wages of sin is death."* Here, we learn that the consequence of living a life of sin is death. Everyone will experience physical death as a result of the sin committed in the garden of Eden, but those who commit themselves to a life of sin will suffer eternal damnation in the lake of fire (Rev. 19).

Continue with the rest of verse 6:23 that says, *"but the gift of God is eternal life through Jesus Christ our Lord."* There is an alternative to suffering eternal damnation. We can accept the gift of salvation by accepting Jesus as our personal lord and savior. Then, Romans 5:8 says, *"But God commendeth his love toward us, in that, while we were yet sinners, Christ died for us."* We are able to receive the gift of salvation because Christ came to earth and shed His blood for us on the cross.

Continue to Romans 10: 9-10 which says, *"That if thou shalt confess with thy mouth the Lord Jesus, and shalt believe in thine heart that God hath raised him from the dead, thou shalt be saved. For with the heart man believeth unto righteousness; and with the mouth confession is made unto salvation."* If we confess with our mouths that Jesus is the son of God, that he came and died for our sins, and that God raised Him from the dead, we will receive salvation.

Finish with Romans 10:13, which states, *"For whosoever shall call upon the name of the Lord shall be saved."* Call upon the name of God by saying these words, "**Lord Jesus, come into my heart and save me**

Lord. I believe that you are the Son of God who came and died on the cross for my sins. I believe that you rose from the grave. I also believe that you now sit in heaven on the right side of the Father, making intersession for me. I accept you as my Lord and my Savior."

Now that you have confessed with your mouth that Jesus is the son of God and that He died for our sins and rose from the grave, **YOU ARE NOW SAVED!!!!** You will spend your eternity in heaven.

The next step is very important- you must find a Bible-based church that teaches the word of God and confesses the Lord Jesus Christ to be the son of God. Don't delay. Do this immediately. Do not leave yourself open to the enemy. Get connected with the saints of the Most High God and keep yourself covered with the unspotted blood of the lamb.

Here is my prayer for you.
Father God,

I thank you for the opportunity to minister your word to the unsaved, the unchurched, and the uncommitted. Father God, I pray now for the souls who have just received the gift of salvation. Lord Father, they have opened their hearts to you, and I know that you have received them into your kingdom and written their names in the Book of Life. Father God, I pray that you will touch their lives and show yourself mightily before them. Let their eyes be opened by the scales falling off, allowing them to see clearly.

Father God, I even pray for the backslider, those who have turned away from you after receiving the gift of salvation. You said in your word that you desire that none would perish. So Lord, I send your word to them right now praying that they would confess the iniquity in their heart, repent, and turn from their evil ways, so that they may receive a life of abundance. You said in your word in Matthew Chapter 14, that every knee shall bow before you and every tongue will confess that Jesus is Lord.

Father God, I pray now that we all come under subjection to your word and that we will humbly submit our lives to you. I ask all these things in the name of my Lord and Savior Jesus Christ.
Amen, Amen, Amen!!!!

I will continue to pray for your success in your walk with God. Remember, this spiritual walk that you are about to embark on will not be an easy walk, but remember, the race is not given to the swift but to those who endure to the end.

Be blessed with heaven's best. I love you!

ABOUT THE AUTHOR

Dr. Cassundra White-Elliott resides in California with her family, where as an English/Education professor she works for various community colleges and universities.

When writing, she writes with the direction of the Holy Spirit, in an effort to share with God's people all that He has for them.

In addition to teaching and writing, Dr. White-Elliott also serves as an evangelistic teacher. She is also the founder of International Women's Commission, a ministry that serves the needs of the entire person, by attending to healing the mind, body, soul, and spirit.

Dr. White-Elliott holds a Ph.D. in Education, a Master's in English Composition, and a Bachelor's in Education.

Dr. White-Elliott is also the founder of CLF Publishing, LLC. For your publishing needs, go online to www.clfpublishing.org.

Daughter, God Loves You!

OTHER BOOKS BY THE AUTHOR

(All books can be purchased at www.creativemindsbookstore.com)

Daughter, God Loves You!

From Despair, through Determination, to Victory!

A lot can happen during a span of 40 years. The life of Dr. Cassundra White-Elliott has been anything but uneventful. From a fun-loving childhood sprinkled with incidents of abuse to a tumultuous young adulthood to a stable, secure adult life, she has experienced a full life, with much more to come. Her story is inspiring and motivating.

If anyone lacks hope, reading Dr. White-Elliott's autobiography will propel him/her into an attitude of "Maybe I can." This attitude, if nurtured and developed, will grow into an attitude of "Yes, I can." Throughout her life, Cassundra has always held in her heart the belief that she could achieve anything that she had a made-up mind to embark upon. She was determined to achieve her heart's desires, doing what God has called her to do. She takes no credit for herself. All the glory goes to God, for He is her driving force. In Him, she lives, moves, and has her being.

Through the Storm

Through the Storm was duly inspired by the avaricious cloud of depression that decided to hover overhead of my daily existence in the latter part of 2007. Although I found it extremely difficult, I was once again compelled to not be defeated by just another snare that the enemy, the trickster, set for me. Once again, or more appropriately I should say *continuously*, he has exerted pernicious efforts to snatch the very life out of me by causing me to wallow in despair and to believe that I had been overcome by failure when in actuality and all reality, I was just experiencing a temporary setback. During those cloudy days, I had to remind myself daily that even though I was a target of the enemy, I am and will always be a child of the Most High god, Jehovah, who is my rock, my stability.

Unleashed Anger, Anger Unleashed

Introduction
What Is This Book All About?

As I prepared to embark upon the adventure of writing this book, I had to prepare myself to also be transparent. I have found that being transparent is required in order for healing to transpire, healing for all those that peruse the pages of this book and myself. And I may as well tell you that today, at the onset of this project, I have not been totally delivered from my condition of being an anger-filled person. However, I am definitely a work in progress. I have made strides with the assistance of my Lord and Savior, Jesus Christ, who is the head of my life. Without his love, guidance, and teachings, I would not be the woman of God I am today. I shudder to think where I could be instead and will therefore not entertain the thought.

Public Speaking in the Spiritual Arena

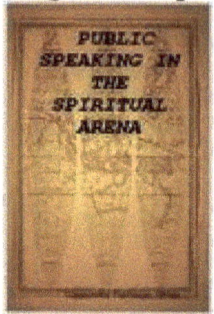

Chapter Two
How Communication Works

Purpose: This chapter will explain the six primary components of communication, identifying their purpose and how they work together.

<u>The Source</u>

In oral communication, the source of information is the speaker. In a church setting, the foundation of the message is God's word, but it is a speaker's interpretation of God's word that is delivered to the audience. As speakers vary, the information may vary but should have a similar essence because the foundational text is the same.

<u>The Message</u>

The message is the collective set of ideas that the speaker (the source) wants to deliver and/or illustrate to the audience. The message can be informative where the speaker informs the audience about a specific set of information. Or, the message may be persuasive in nature if the speaker wants to persuade the audience about conducting themselves in a specific manner, accepting God's commandments, or any number of things.

Where is Your Joppa?

Introduction

Where is Your Joppa? was written for the express purpose of illustrating God's call for obedience in the lives of believers with respect to the individual call that He has on each of our lives. As you read throughout the various chapters, notice that the emphasis is placed on our persistent disobedience in answering God's call in a specific area of our lives. We have become a people who are similar to the Israelites when they found themselves in the middle of the wilderness, following their exodus from Egypt. Before God, they murmured and complained about their current life conditions and failed to be obedient to God's statutes delivered through His servant Moses. Their persistent disobedience caused them to lose the opportunity to see and enter the Promised Land. I ask you, "What has your disobedience cost you?" "Was your disobedience worth what it cost you?" "Do you think about the souls you could have ushered into the kingdom of God?" These are some of the questions that I pray will be answered through your reading of the book.

Mayhem in the Hamptons

Romero and Yolanda optimistically plan for the day that is going to change their lives from being single persons to a couple who is united in holy matrimony. They, along with their parents, close friends and family, fly over to the infamous Hamptons, where only the rich and famous vacation, to have their dream wedding at the five-star Hampton Suites located on a peninsula in the Hamptons. Little do they know that their perfect day will turn out to be less than perfect when their wedding planner Mariesha Coleman suddenly goes missing!

A time when the newlyweds' lives should be filled with joy and the creation of wonderful memories, they are stricken with grief as they desperately try to find clues to help solve Mariesha's disappearance.

Mayhem in the Hamptons is a tale that shares how the horrors of a woman's past can come back to haunt her in more than one way and the impact it can have on anyone who gets in the way.

Preacher's Daughter

Tinisha, the daughter of a preacher, is a twenty-six year old God-fearing young woman endeavoring to complete law school so that she can make her mark in the courtroom. Working in one of the late-night clubs in Hollywood to earn money to pay her own way through school, Tinisha soon learns that life doesn't always go as planned. Finding her strength in her faith, Tinisha constantly finds herself praying as she watches God move miraculously in her life.

Preacher's Son

Romero Turner is a private investigator with a promising future. As he continues to build his career, he is excited about the cases he undertakes. However, his father Pastor Theodore Turner has other plans for his son's life. In the midst of trying to save his client's husband from Sylvester Domingo, a ruthless crime lord, Romero must try to salvage his relationship with his father. He must decide if ministry or life as a detective is in his future.

Lord, Teach Me to be a Blessing!

Lord, Teach Me to be a Blessing! will change a person's mentality from being centered around "me, myself, and I" to focusing on "others."

The world system teaches us that it is acceptable to place ourselves above others in an attempt to get ahead and even to survive. Herbert Spencer coined the phrase '*survival of the fittest*' after reading Charles Darwin's theory of evolution. This concept of surpassing and outdoing others is the world's philosophy.

However, the word of God does not subscribe to or promote this self-centered ideology, and therefore, neither should believers. We must hold fast to the truths outlined in Holy Scripture: "*Love thy neighbor as you love thyself*" (James 2:8) and "*It is more blessed to give than to receive*" (Acts 20:35). While holding God's truths to be self-evident, we must demonstrate them to others, thereby showing them the way of the Lord of how to be a blessing to someone *rather* than looking to receive a blessing.
This is the very purpose of this book: to change the mentality of the world from being *self*-centered to *other* centered.

After the Dust Settles

Throughout the journey of life, we all experience ups and downs and joys and pains. Most of us successfully find solutions to the situations/problems we encounter, but we often avoid dealing with the attached emotions. If we continue to ignore the emotions of pain, hurt, disappointment, anger, etc., we set ourselves up for destruction. Our families, our cultures, and our society tell us to be strong, to keep our chin up, and to grin and bear it. However, these methods of avoidance can lead us to strokes due to the undue amount of pressure we place on ourselves and/or mental illness from being unable to cope with the emotional baggage we have accumulated.

In *After the Dust Settles,* Dr. C. White-Elliott shares several situations that we all may encounter at one time or another in our lifetime and how to successfully navigate through them, so we can find ourselves emotionally healthy after the dust has settled and the situation has been rectified.

Begin reading today and experience a better tomorrow!

A Diamond in the Rough

A Diamond in the Rough Architecture Firm was built and is owned and operated by lead architect Kyra Fraser. For the last five years, Kyra has been extremely successful in business, but her love life leaves much to be desired.

Kyra has set high standards for herself and does not wish to take a man in any condition and attempt to make him over. She is looking for someone who is drama free, well educated, very cultured, fun-loving, good looking, self-motivated, and the list goes on.

Will Kyra find the man of her dreams, or will her dream just continue to be a dream?

As you delve into this page-turning novel, Kyra's reality will unfold as you are drawn into her world of design, love and office drama- which includes her best friend's husband who is looking for love in all the wrong places.

365 Days of Encouragement

Just as our brain requires oxygen obtained from the air we breathe to sustain our mortal bodies, our spirit requires revitalization and encouragement in order to be strengthened each and every day of our lives. The revitalization and encouragement needed for the spirit of man comes directly from the word of God and assists us in walking according to the way of our heavenly Father. 365 Days of Encouragement provides a scripture a day for each day of the year. Along with the daily scripture is a brief note of commentary also for the benefit of edifying the saints of God.

It is my prayer that the people of God would live a fulfilled life through Christ Jesus. Knowing His word and understanding we can walk in the fulfillment thereof is empowering. We are instructed in II Timothy 2:15, "Study to shew thyself approved unto God, a workman that needeth not to be ashamed, rightly dividing the word of truth" (KJV). Take an opportunity to delve further into the word of God, to know His statutes and to allow your own personal life to be edified, so you can be equipped to bring glory to God and lived a fulfilled life.

A Mother's Heart

A Mother's Heart shares the unconditional love of mothers through a compilation of testimonies. Each testimony serves as a tribute to a special mother. The children of the represented mothers have lovingly written about their childhood, young adult life and/or older adult experiences they shared with their mother. As you read the writers' reflections, you will feel the expressions of love exude from the pages.

The purpose of this book is two-fold. First, it honors those mothers who stood by their children through the trials of life and showered them with unconditional love. Second, the book is a source of encouragement for mothers who may feel inadequate and question whether or not they are actually suited for motherhood. Our advice to mothers is, "Be encouraged; the journey of motherhood may seem daunting at times and you may shed some tears, but your children will never forget the love you have shown them and instilled in them to share with others."

Mothers may not be perfect, but they are definitely unmatched by any other category of person on God's green earth!

Broken Chains

Broken Chains is an in-depth survey of five life-changing tragedies that can and will serve as chains to bind us if we are not watchful and mindful of their potential effects. In our lifetimes, we may all experience death of loved ones, sexual abuse, broken relationships, promiscuity, and sickness and disease. These everyday life occurrences can have detrimental effects on the remaining years of our lives and change our existence, unless we deal with them in a healthy manner.

Broken Chains not only brings to light the detrimental effects of five life-changing tragedies, but it also shares how anyone who experiences them can be healed and delivered from their effects.

If you have experienced death of a loved one, sexual abuse, a broken relationship, the effects of promiscuity, and/or sickness and disease and have not been able to rid yourself of the emotions attached to them or specific resulting behaviors, Broken Chains is for you.

God designed each of us for a purpose, and He has an intended end for us to achieve. In order for us to effectively achieve our God-given purpose, we must be free of chains that bind us. It is not God's desire that we become immobilized by life's events. His desire is for us to be healed, delivered and set free. Be healed today, in the name of the Lord Jesus Christ!

I Have Fallen

Do you know anyone who has committed his/her life to Christ but has done something unseemly that you would never expect a Christian to do? How did you feel about that person or what the person did? Did you pass judgment? What if that person were you? How would you feel if you made a misstep and no one forgave you and instead began to treat you differently? How do you feel when you are judged for past mistakes or lifestyles that are no longer part of your life?

This book shares four true stories of Christians who have made missteps during their walk with God. The purpose is not to air their dirty laundry, but to demonstrate our humanness and our vulnerability. None of us are exempt from making errors and falling into sin. It can happen to any of us.

The solution for these dilemmas is for the person who fell into sin to make a life-changing move and turn away from the sin, repent and ask God for forgiveness. His arms are waiting!

The next solution is for those who witness the sin or know of it. Pray and be of comfort to the one who has fallen. Lead him/her back to the path of righteousness. Love thy neighbor and treat him/her as you want to be treated!

The Bottom Line

The Bottom Line is a detailed review of the Book of Job. Much can be said about Job's experiences with the loss of his children and wealth and the subsequent return of it all in mass proportions. However, the telling of Job's story in the Holy writ was not intended to focus on the return of his wealth. Instead, the focal point should be on the bottom line of the entire situation.

When you experience trials or tragedies in your life, do you tend to focus on the trial itself, the result, or the bottom line?

"What is the bottom line?" you may ask. The bottom line is the message God is sending regarding the situation.

When Job experienced his tragedies, there was a bottom line. Likewise, when you experience your trials and tragedies, there is a bottom line as well. It is up to you to discover it.

This book will reveal the bottom line in the Book of Job. It is readily apparent, but many often overlook it.

Now, it is up to you to uncover the bottom line of your experiences, for God will not bring a trial to you without a good reason.

Power of a Woman

The ongoing conversation about the value of a woman is presented from a different perspective in The Power of a Woman. Dr. Cassundra White-Elliott presents a biblical perspective of women and compares it to the worldview of both yesterday and today. This comparison seeks to illustrate God's intended purpose for His uniquely designed creation: woman. Dr. Elliott shares God's truth about pre-imposed limitations set by man versus the limitations God Himself set for woman in addition to the wealth of liberality He gave her.

Women's creativity and abilities are not meant to be stifled. They are meant to be utilized to bring glory to God, to help sustain and nurture their families, and to move the world forward. Knowing God's truth will show women how to celebrate and appreciate who they are as well as one another!

Women, let's take the blinders off, lift our heads up, and march forward, side by side with men, and bring glory and honor to God! Take your rightful place with a gentle smile and grace and be who God called you to be!

Set Free

If you possess habits and display characteristics that are unbecoming, debilitating, and hinder the desired progress in your life or that affect your relationships with others, Set Free will provide the steps you need to be healed and delivered, through the Word of God.

Deliverance is available to you! Claim your healing today and walk in victory!

Do You Know God?

Have you or someone you know ever felt alone, confused, or unsure about your walk with God or are you unsure of what being a Christian is all about? *Do You Know God?* is an excellent text for providing answers to many of your questions. This book introduces adolescents and young adults to God in addition to answer many of their questions about being a Christian. This book shares the testimonies of the trials and tribulations that other teens have experienced and how God prevailed in their lives. All the information that is shared on the pages of the book is based upon the Word of God and the scriptures are taken from the King James Version of the Bible. If you are interested in knowing more about God's Word or how to begin your Christian experience, this book is for you.

www.ingramcontent.com/pod-product-compliance
Lightning Source LLC
LaVergne TN
LVHW010315070426
835510LV00024B/3393